ABORTION BAN

FROM THE

MOMENT OF FERTILIZATION:

A BLATANT ATTACK ON WOMEN'S REPRODUCTIVE RIGHTS

JENNY ROBINS

INTRODUCTION

HOW TO REDUCE ABORTION THE RIGHT WAY

INTRODUCTION

Claire Malone, an Irish mother with two children, presented her traumatic story with Amnesty International Ireland on how her right to health was jeopardized by her inability to have an abortion due to the country's severe abortion laws.

Claire was diagnosed with pulmonary atresia and pulmonary hypertension in 2014, and her lung was removed. Women with pulmonary hypertension are at a high risk of getting even more critically unwell or dying during pregnancy if they become pregnant. Claire is well aware of this, which is why she requested a termination, which was denied by her doctors due to legal restrictions.

"My doctors told me they couldn't offer me a termination because my life wasn't in danger at the time, and that was the end of it." I am aware that they are legally bound. But I believed that if I waited until my health deteriorated to the point where I could die, it would be too late. And why is a threat to my health, which was already grave, insufficient? How much more must I endure before my physicians are permitted to treat me?"

If performed according to WHO guidelines, abortion is one of the safest medical treatments available. When it is conducted with an unsafe method, however, it causes at least one in every six maternal deaths due to complications. In 2004, WHO conducted research based on estimations and data from all countries and found that the more legal grounds for abortion are expanded, the fewer fatalities from unsafe abortions occur. The study found that in most countries, only six main reasons for allowing abortion apply:

1 - Death threat

2 – Sexual assault or rape

3 – Severe prenatal abnormality

4 – Physical and sometimes mental health hazards

5 – Economic and social factors

6 – On-demand

The statistics reveal that as you get from ground 1 to ground 6, the number of deaths decreases. Countries that allow abortion on demand without restrictions have nearly no deaths from unsafe abortion. This is proof that removing all legal restrictions and providing universal access to safe abortion is the best way to consign unsafe abortion to history. However, the question remains as to how we get from where we are now to where we could (and should) be.

The transition from almost total illegality of abortion to partial (let alone total) decriminalization has been gradual and challenging. Why? Because (the danger of or otherwise) in pregnancy is the most effective way of controlling the lives of women. Traditional beliefs that women should accept "all the children God gives," modern glorification of the fetus as having more value than the mother on whom it depends, and male-dominated culture are all invoked to justify criminal prohibitions. Nonetheless, one of the distinguishing sensations of having a uterus is the need for abortion.

Induced abortion was used in 25% of pregnancies worldwide from 2010 to 2014, including in countries with high contraceptive prevalence. Several women are defending the need for abortion, as well as the right to safe abortion, and access to it if and when they need it, thanks to years of non-stop activism. Furthermore, an increasing number of governments, both in the Global North and, more recently, in the Global South, have begun to recognize that preventing unsafe abortions is in line with their commitment to reducing avoidable maternal deaths and their duty under international human rights law.

While some individuals still believe that this may be accomplished just through increased contraceptive usage or post-abortion care, the data show that this is not the case. Both contraceptive failure and failure to take contraception are common events and sexual practices.

The Oklahoma legislature's bill prohibits almost all abortions.

The law outlaws abortion from the moment of fertilization and is enforced by private civil litigation.

Oklahoma has been at the forefront of a wave of Republican-led states rushing to adopt abortion-related legislation in the hope that the Supreme Court will overturn Roe v. Wade shortly.

On Thursday, May 19, 2022, the Oklahoma Legislature gave final approval to a bill prohibiting nearly all abortions beginning at fertilization, making it the nation's harshest abortion ban. The bill allows individuals to sue abortion providers as well as anyone who "aids or abets" an abortion. If signed by Republican Gov. Kevin Stitt, who has pledged to make Oklahoma the most anti-abortion state in the country, it would take effect immediately.

On the 19th of May 2022, State Representative Jim Olsen, a Republican, opined on the floor of the Oklahoma House, "There can be nothing higher or more vital than the safeguarding of innocent, unborn life."

The bill is based on Texas legislation that went into effect in September 2021, prohibiting abortion beyond six weeks and relying on civil rather than criminal enforcement to avoid judicial challenges. Because of that provision, the law expressly states that state authorities cannot bring charges, and the United States Supreme Court and state courts have said they cannot overturn the ban, even if it violates Roe v. Wade's constitutional right to abortion. The Oklahoma bill goes further than the Texas statute, which prohibits abortion after six weeks. "A human fetus or embryo in any stage of gestation from conception to birth," according to its definition of an unborn child. Since the Roe v. Wade decision in 1973, anti-abortion groups have tried unsuccessfully to pass federal or state legislation defining life as beginning at fertilization.

The vote on Thursday was the latest step by Oklahoma's Republican-led Legislature, which has been working to whittle away at abortion rights until it is effectively outlawed. Together, they have propelled their state to the forefront of the pack of Republican-led states rushing to adopt abortion-related legislation in the hope that the Supreme Court would soon overturn Roe v. Wade.

Outnumbered Democrats in Oklahoma's State House begged their colleagues not to vote for the bill on Thursday. Several people advocated for Oklahoma to prioritize financing for family planning services or improving the lives of poor young Oklahomans.

The bill contains an exception for situations of rape and incest, but only if police enforcement has been notified. Oklahoma already has a trigger ban that will prohibit abortion immediately if the Supreme Court overturns Roe, as well as an abortion ban that has been in place since before Roe. If signed by the governor, the Oklahoma bill would eliminate another option for Texas women seeking legal abortions, and it would punish even individuals from out of state who help Oklahoma women obtain abortions. The current bill in Oklahoma was denounced by the Biden administration as the most extreme example of politicians restricting access to abortion.

Other states have attempted to outlaw abortions throughout pregnancy, but have been blocked by a court ruling since, under the Roe decision, states cannot prohibit abortion until viability, which is approximately 24 weeks. Mississippi has tried but failed to pass ballot propositions that would classify fetuses as persons and make abortion murder.

At the moment, no state restricts abortion after conception. The Oklahoma bill tries to accomplish so by using a legal method that the courts have approved: civilian enforcement.

1

ABORTION AND THE KEY FACTS AROUND IT

Abortion

A medical operation that terminates a pregnancy is known as an abortion. For millions of women, girls, and others who may become pregnant, it is a basic healthcare requirement. Every year, about one in every four pregnancies ends in an abortion. While the need for abortion is common, those who require abortion services do not always have access to safe and legal abortion services.

In truth, abortion access is one of the most contentious issues in the world, with disinformation about the true consequences of restricting access to this vital healthcare service clouding the debate.

Abortion is a regular medical procedure. It is safe when done according to WHO guidelines, according to the length of the pregnancy, and by someone with the requisite abilities.

Induced abortions occur in six out of ten unintended pregnancies. Approximately 45 percent of all abortions are unsafe, with 97 percent occurring in developing countries. Unsafe abortion is a primary cause of maternal mortality and morbidity, but it can be avoided. It can cause physical and mental health problems, as well as social and financial hardships for women, communities, and health care systems. A crucial public health and human rights issue is the lack of safe, timely, cheap, and respectful abortion care.

Consequences of being unable to obtain high-quality abortion care

Women's physical and mental health is jeopardized throughout their lives due to a lack of safe, inexpensive, timely, and respectful abortion care, as well as the stigma associated with abortion.

The right to life, the right to the highest attainable standard of physical and mental health, the right to benefit from scientific progress and its realization, the right to decide freely and responsibly on the number, spacing, and timing of children, and the right to be free from torture, cruel, inhuman, and degrading treatment and punishment are all at risk if quality abortion care is unavailable.

Unsafe abortion is responsible for 4.7–13.2 percent of maternal deaths every year. In developed and rich countries, 30 women are predicted to die for every 100,000 unsafe abortions. In countries that are not developed, the fatality rate climbs to 220 per 100,000 unsafe abortions.

Incomplete abortion (failure to remove or expel all pregnancy tissue from the uterus); Hemorrhage (severe bleeding); Infection; Uterine perforation (caused when the uterus is punctured by a sharp item); and Uterine perforation (induced when the uterus is penetrated by a sharp object); Inserting harmful things into the vagina or anus causes damage to the genital system and internal organs.

Restrictive abortion regulations can cause distress and stigma, as well as a violation of women's and girls' human rights, such as the right to privacy and the right to non-discrimination and equality, as well as financial difficulties. Regulations that require women to travel to obtain legal care, or that mandate mandatory counseling or waiting periods, result in lost wages and other financial expenditures and can make abortion unavailable to women with limited resources.

According to several reviews from 2021, abortion rules affect the education of women, productive labor market engagement, and positive contribution to GDP growth through being connected to fertility. The legal status of abortion can have an impact on children's educational outcomes as well as their future wages on the job market. If abortion is legalized, for example, it can lead to increased parental investments in children, notably in girls' education, by reducing the incidence of undesired pregnancies and therefore raising the possibility that children are born wanted.

Increasing access to high-quality abortion services

Restricting abortion access does not affect the number of abortions performed; however, it does affect whether the abortions performed on women and girls are safe and dignified. In nations with severe abortion restrictions, the proportion of unsafe abortions is much higher than in countries with less strict rules.

High prices, the stigma for people seeking abortions and healthcare professionals, and healthcare workers' unwillingness to administer an abortion based on personal conscience or religious belief are all barriers to safe and respectful abortion. Restrictive laws and requirements that are not medically justified, such as the criminalization of abortion, mandatory waiting periods, biased information or counseling, third-party authorization, and restrictions on the types of health care providers or facilities that can provide abortion services, further limit access.

Basic Facts About Abortion

ABORTIONS OCCUR ALL THE TIME, NO MATTER WHAT THE LAW SAYS.

Abortion is a frequent decision made by millions of people each year, with one-quarter of pregnancies ending in abortion. Regardless of whether abortion is legal or not, individuals still require and use abortion services regularly. According to findings, the abortion rate is 37 per

1,000 people in countries that restrict abortion entirely or allow it only in emergency situations to save a woman's life, and 34 per 1,000 people in countries that allow abortion generally, a statistically insignificant difference.

Abortions are one of the safest medical operations known, even safer than childbirth when performed by a competent healthcare practitioner in sanitary settings. People are forced to resort to clandestine, risky abortions when governments restrict abortion access, particularly those who cannot afford to fly or seek private care. This leads to my next point.

CRIMINALISING ABORTION DOESN'T PREVENT ABORTION; IT JUST MAKES IT LESS SAFE.

Stopping women and girls from having abortions does not mean they no longer need them. That is why banning or restricting abortions does not have any effect on the number of abortions done; instead, it forces people to seek out dangerous abortions. The World Health Organization (WHO) defines unsafe abortions as "a procedure for terminating an unplanned pregnancy carried out either by personnel lacking the essential skills or in a setting that does not meet minimum medical standards or both."

They estimate that 25 million illegal abortions occur each year, with the vast majority occurring in underdeveloped nations. Unsafe abortions, in contrast to legal abortions performed by a trained medical physician, can result in death. According to the World Health Organization, unsafe abortions are the third biggest cause of maternal deaths globally and inflict an extra five million completely preventable impairments.

ALMOST EVERY DEATH AND INJURY CAUSED BY UNSAFE ABORTION IS AVOIDABLE.

Abortion-related deaths and injuries can be avoided. Yet, in countries where access to safe abortion is restricted or forbidden outright, such deaths are prevalent, as the majority of women and girls who require an abortion due to an undesired pregnancy are unable to do so legally.

In countries with such restrictions, the law usually allows for so-called "limited exceptions" to the anti-abortion legislation. These exclusions may apply when the pregnancy is the result of rape or incest, in circumstances of severe and fatal fetal damage, or when the pregnant person's life or health is at risk. Because these reasons account for a small number of abortions, the majority of women and girls living under these rules may be forced to seek unsafe abortions, putting their health and lives at risk.

Those who are already marginalized are disproportionately harmed by such regulations because they lack the financial resources to seek safe and legal services in another nation or to pay for private care. Women and girls from low-income families, refugees and migrants, teenagers, lesbians, bisexuals, cisgender women and girls, transgender or gender non-conforming people, and women from minority or Indigenous groups are among them.

One of the first measures in preventing maternal fatalities and injuries, according to the WHO, is for states to ensure that people have access to sex education, effective contraception, safe and legal abortion, and timely care for complications.

Abortion rates are higher in countries with poor contraception access, according to research. Abortion rates are lower in areas where people, including adolescents, have access to and knowledge of modern contraceptive methods, as well as comprehensive sexuality education and safe and legal abortion on broad grounds.

MANY COUNTRIES ARE BEGINNING TO AMEND THEIR LAWS TO ALLOW FOR EASIER ABORTION ACCESS.

More than 50 nations have amended their laws to allow for wider abortion access in the last 25 years, recognizing the critical role that safe abortion plays in preserving women's lives and health. On May 25, 2018, Ireland's people overwhelmingly chose to repeal the near-total constitutional ban on abortion in a long-awaited referendum.

Despite the trend toward modifying laws to prevent deaths and injuries, certain nations, such as Nicaragua and El Salvador, continue to have harsh and discriminatory abortion laws that prohibit abortion in almost all instances. According to the WHO, 40% of women of reproductive age live in countries with extremely restrictive abortion legislation, or in countries where abortion is legal but not available or accessible. Abortion is illegal or only permitted in very limited circumstances in certain states, or if legal, it is not available due to many impediments to access in practice.

Even in jurisdictions where legal abortion is more widely available, pregnant women may face a variety of restrictions and impediments to care, including cost, biased counseling, and obligatory waiting periods. States have been given technical instructions by the WHO on how to identify and eliminate such impediments.

ABORTION CRIMINALISATION OR RESTRICTION PREVENTS DOCTORS FROM PROVIDING BASIC CARE.

Health-care practitioners are prevented from doing their jobs effectively and offering the greatest care alternatives for their patients due to criminalization and restrictive abortion regulations, which is contrary to sound medical practice and their professional ethical duties.

The criminalization of abortion has a "chilling effect," in which medical personnel may not understand the legal boundaries or may apply the limitations more narrowly than the law requires. This could be due to a variety of factors, such as personal convictions, abortion stigma, bad perceptions about women and girls, or the fear of criminal culpability.

It also discourages women and girls from seeking post-abortion care for problems resulting from an unsafe abortion or other pregnancy-related issues.

ABORTIONS ARE NOT ONLY REQUIRED FOR CISGENDER WOMEN AND GIRLS.

Intersex persons, transgender men and boys, and people with alternative gender identities may need abortion services, as well as cisgender women and girls (women and girls who were designated female at birth).

Lack of access to healthcare is one of the most significant barriers to abortion access for these persons and groups. Those who do have access to healthcare may also encounter stigma and biased attitudes from healthcare providers, as well as assumptions that they do not require contraception or abortion-related information and treatments. In other situations, 28 percent of transgender and gender-nonconforming people say they've been harassed in medical settings, and 19 percent say they've been denied medical care because of their gender identity, with significantly higher proportions among people of color. This is due to several interconnected issues such as poverty and race, as well as related intersectional discrimination.

Sexual and reproductive rights advocates and LGBTI rights activists are working to raise awareness about this issue and to make abortion services available, accessible, and inclusive to everyone who needs them, regardless of their sexual orientation or gender identity.

ABORTION CRIMINALISATION IS A TYPE OF DISCRIMINATION THAT FURTHER FUELS STIGMA.

To begin with, discrimination occurs when medical treatments, particularly reproductive health services, are denied to only certain persons.

Restrictive abortion laws are discriminatory against women, according to the United Nations Committee on the Elimination of All Forms of Discrimination Against Women (CEDAW, or the Treaty on the Rights of Women). This includes discrimination against lesbians, bisexuals, and/or transgender women, especially given the specific forms of gendered discrimination they face, as the CEDAW Committee has confirmed that CEDAW's protections, and states' related obligations, apply to all women, including lesbians, bisexuals, and/or transgender women.

Second, the criminalization of abortion and other restrictive abortion laws and regulations are inextricably tied to abortion stigma and gender stereotyping. Women and girls are stigmatized by health care workers, family members, and the judiciary, among others, simply because they believe abortion is illegal or unethical. As a result, women and girls seeking abortion face harassment and prejudice. When seeking abortion services or post-abortion care, several women have reported being assaulted and degraded by health care workers.

HUMAN RIGHTS REQUIRE ACCESS TO SAFE ABORTION.

It is a human right to have access to safe abortion services. Under international human rights law, everyone has a right to life, a right to health, and a right to be free from violence, discrimination, and torture or cruel, inhuman, and degrading treatment. Bodily autonomy is defined by human rights legislation as the ability to make decisions about your body on your own.

Forcing someone to carry on an unwanted pregnancy or seek an unsafe abortion violates their human rights, including their right to privacy and bodily autonomy. Those who have no choice but to resort to unsafe abortions face prosecution and punishment, including incarceration, as well as harsh, inhuman, and humiliating treatment and discrimination in post-abortion health care, as well as exclusion from it.

Abortion access is thus inextricably related to the protection and upholding of the human rights of women, girls, and those who may become pregnant, and hence to achieving social and gender justice. Amnesty International believes that everyone should be able to exercise their bodily autonomy and make their own reproductive decisions, including when and whether or not to have children. It is critical that abortion regulations respect, protect, and fulfill the human rights of pregnant women, rather than forcing them to seek out hazardous abortions.

2

LEGACY OF ROE V. WADE

Roe v. Wade was a historic legal decision delivered by the United States Supreme Court on January 22, 1973, in which the court overturned a Texas law prohibiting abortion, essentially legalizing the operation throughout the United States. The court decided that a woman's right to an abortion was implicit in the 14th Amendment's right to privacy. Before Roe v. Wade, abortion had been banned in most of the United States since the late 1800s. Many states have implemented restrictions on abortion rights since the 1973 judgment.

Abortion was permitted in the United States until the late 19th century, before "quickening," the period at which a woman can first feel movements of the fetus, usually around the fourth month of pregnancy.

Early abortion rules were implemented in the 1820s and 1830s, and they dealt with the selling of harmful medications used by women to induce abortions. Despite these restrictions and the reality that the medications may kill women, they were still advertised and sold.

The newly formed American Medical Association began lobbying for the criminalization of abortion in the late 1850s, partly to eliminate doctors' competitors like midwives and homeopaths.

Furthermore, some nativists were anti-abortion because they anticipated decreased birth rates among white, American-born, Protestant women, who were worried by the country's expanding number of immigrants.

The Catholic Church outlawed abortion at any stage of pregnancy in 1869, and Congress passed the Comstock Act in 1873, making it illegal to mail contraceptives and abortion-inducing medications in the United States. Abortion was illegal in much of the country by the 1880s. Court battles addressing contraception in the 1960s, during the women's rights movement, lay the framework for Roe v. Wade.

The United States Supreme Court knocked down a regulation prohibiting married couples from receiving birth control in 1965, saying that the law violated their implied right to privacy under the US Constitution. A law prohibiting the delivery of contraceptives to unmarried persons was knocked down by the Supreme Court in 1972.

Meanwhile, Hawaii became the first state to allow abortion in 1970, though only for residents of the state. New York also legalized abortion in the same year, with no residence requirements. Abortion was legal in Alaska and Washington at the time Roe v. Wade was decided in 1973.

Norma McCorvey, a Texas lady in her early twenties, was seeking to end an undesired pregnancy in 1969. McCorvey had previously given birth twice and given both children up for adoption, despite growing up in terrible, destitute conditions. Abortion was permitted in Texas at the time of McCorvey's pregnancy in 1969—but only if the woman's life was in danger.

While wealthy American women could go to foreign countries where abortions were safe and legal, or pay a substantial sum to a U.S. doctor willing to perform an abortion in secret, McCorvey and many other women were unable to take advantage of these possibilities.

As a result, some women have turned to illegal, sometimes deadly "back-alley" abortions or self-induced abortions. According to the Guttmacher Institute, the number of illegal abortions in the United States varied from 200,000 to 1.2 million per year in the 1950s and 1960s.

After failing to have an illegal abortion, McCorvey was recommended to Texas attorneys Linda Coffee and Sarah Weddington, who were interested in fighting anti-abortion legislation. McCorvey was dubbed "Jane Roe" in court records.

In 1970, the attorneys filed a lawsuit against Henry Wade, the district attorney of Dallas County, on behalf of McCorvey and all other women "who were or might become pregnant and desire to examine all options." Wade had previously made global headlines in 1964 when he prosecuted Jack Ruby, the man accused of assassinating President John F. Kennedy.

A Texas district court found in June 1970 that the state's abortion ban was unconstitutional because it infringed on a fundamental right to privacy. Following that, Wade stated that he will continue to punish doctors who perform abortions. The matter was finally taken to the United States Supreme Court. Meanwhile, McCovey had a baby and placed it for adoption.

Roe v. Wade, 410 U.S. 113, transformed the legal position of abortion in 1973 by overturning a Texas law that made abortion illegal unless it was used to save the mother's life. Individual privacy rights were set against the state's need to regulate the life of the fetus in this case. The Court decided that a woman's autonomy and reproductive rights extend to her decision to terminate her pregnancy, based on the Due Process Clause of the Fourteenth Amendment and the Right to Privacy guaranteed by the Ninth Amendment. The Court ruled that the state's interest in the fetus became significant only after the fetus reached "viability," or the point at which it could survive without its mother. Government bans on abortion were confined to post-viability interventions, and the state could never put the fetus' life ahead of the mother's. States' pre-viability abortion regulation was restricted by a woman's freedom to terminate her pregnancy. The "trimester formula" established by Justice Blackmun rooted the concept of viability and created a timetable by which states may lawfully restrict abortion. Roe did not allow abortion in all cases, but it did strike a balance between the states' interest in the fetus' life and women's privacy rights.

The court separated pregnancy into three trimesters and decided that the woman had sole discretion over whether or not to terminate a pregnancy in the first trimester. To preserve the mother's health, the government could limit, but not prohibit, abortion in the second trimester. The state might restrict abortion in the third trimester to safeguard a fetus that could survive outside the womb unless the woman's health was in jeopardy.

Since Roe v. Wade, numerous states have enacted abortion legislation that specifies the circumstances under which a woman may have an abortion. State abortion laws aimed at narrowing the scope of what is allowable under Roe's broad legal umbrella added fuel to an already smoldering issue. The case of Planned Parenthood of Southeastern Pennsylvania v. Casey, 505 U.S. 833 (1992), in which no majority judgment was written, brought the Roe v. Wade debate into sharp focus. Casey's question is whether five independent limitations imposed by Pennsylvania state law on a woman's right to abortion are constitutional. The Court found three of the five criteria – parental consent, informed consent, and a 24-hour waiting time – constitutionally permissible because they did not excessively burden a woman seeking an abortion, according to the majority judgment written by Justices

O'Connor, Kennedy, and Souter. Spousal notification was declared unlawful because it imposed an "undue hardship." These cases used a new legal criterion, undue burden, created by Justice O'Connor in Akron v. Akron Center for Reproductive Health, Inc., 462 U.S. 416 (1983), as a way of sustaining Roe's main rationale while also restricting its reach without causing women hardship. Casey, which rejected Roe's trimester model, used the concept of viability to bridge the gap between states' interests and women's right to privacy. States, like Roe, could outright prohibit abortion once a fetus reaches viability. Casey declared medical science to be subject to state regulations and mandates, particularly the language and information used by doctors and hospitals in elaborating abortion procedures for patients.

Even though Casey was a big triumph for anti-abortion activists, numerous states continued to implement laws that eroded Roe's main entitlement. In Stenberg v. Carhart, 530 U.S. 914 (2000), the Supreme Court considered a Nebraska legislation that made it illegal to perform a group of treatments known as "partial-birth abortion." The Court concluded that the act, which made no exceptions – not even to protect the mother's health – was a violation of the Fourteenth Amendment's Due Process Clause. When Congress passed the Partial-Birth Abortion Ban Act of 2003, the argument over so-called partial-birth abortion just transferred to the legislative branch. Carhart, one of only a few doctors in the US who conduct third-trimester abortions, sued, claiming that the Act violated the Fifth Amendment's liberty rights by outright prohibiting partial-birth abortions.

The Supreme Court ruled in Gonzales v. Carhart, 550 U.S. 124 (2007), that the law prohibiting abortions described in terms of their method – intact dilation and extraction – did not impose an undue burden on women, create hardship, or otherwise fail to protect their health by effectively preventing access to abortion because such procedures are never medically necessary.

On the same day as Roe, the Supreme Court decided Doe v. Bolton, 410 U.S. 179, which established the concept of health within the jurisdiction of physicians. The Court was asked to rule on a Georgia legislation that prohibited medical abortion unless it was conducted by a licensed physician using his best judgment and to save the mother's life. The Court determined that doctors have privileged knowledge of life and health that qualifies them to assess the risks presented by abortion operations. Doe signified the Court's greatest effort to downplay the political dimension of abortion by arguing that scientific knowledge and practical experience, rather than legislative acts, best suited the interests of women, fetuses, and states in the abortion debate. Doe then alleged privacy protection for the confidential patient-physician connection. In the case of Planned Parenthood of Central Missouri v. Danforth 428 U.S. 52, which ruled "viability" to be a concept properly defined by the medical establishment rather than state governments, physicians' expertise was upheld once more in 1976.

The Supreme Court agreed to hear Dobbs v. Jackson Women's Health Organization, a case challenging the validity of a Mississippi legislation prohibiting most abortions after 15 weeks of pregnancy, in May 2022. Roe v. Wade is directly challenged in this case.

Importance of Roe V Wade

Roe v. Wade is widely regarded as the case that "legalized abortion." However, this isn't entirely accurate. It changed the way states can restrict abortion and defined abortion as a matter of constitutional privacy rights.

It may come as a surprise that Roe had little effect on the number of abortions done in the United States each year. According to the Guttmacher Institute, approximately one million illegal abortions were performed in the United States each year in the years before Roe was established. Following Roe, the number of legally conducted abortions has remained around one million. Furthermore, in the years following Roe, the number of deaths caused by abortions decreased considerably.

Since the Supreme Court's ruling in Roe v. Wade, courts have interpreted the constitution to allow abortion. Many abortion opponents have fought for tougher abortion legislation since Roe. Although opponents have not been successful in outright banning abortions, they have been able to impose restrictions. Several states have put limits on abortions in specific situations, such as parental notification laws, mandatory publication of abortion risk information, and late-term abortion restrictions.

The question has resurfaced in presidential debates and around the country. States continue to establish abortion laws, which are frequently challenged in federal courts. However, just a few people make it to the Supreme Court. Many people are wondering if Roe v. Wade will be reversed.

What If Roe V. Wade Were To Be Overturned?

A major Supreme Court decision, Roe v. Wade, legalized abortion in the United States. On January 22, 1973, the 7-2 decision was announced. The majority ruling was written by Justice Harry A. Blackmun, a modest Midwestern Republican who supports abortion rights. The verdict overturned laws prohibiting abortion in numerous states, stating that they could not prohibit the operation before a fetus can survive outside the womb. When Roe was decided, that point, known as fetal viability, was roughly 28 weeks. Most specialists now believe it will take between 23 and 24 weeks. The case established a foundation for abortion law based on pregnancy trimesters. It allowed essentially little limitations in the first trimester. It allowed measures to protect women's health in the second. Third, it permitted states to prohibit abortions as long as exceptions were granted to safeguard the mother's life and health. In 1992, the Supreme Court overturned that framework while upholding Roe's core holding.

What would happen if the Roe decision was overturned? Individual states would have the authority to decide whether or not abortions are lawful. In nearly half of them, the practice would be outrightly prohibited or severely restricted, although many would continue to accept it. Thirteen states have so-called trigger laws, which make abortion illegal immediately if Roe were overturned.

"This is part of a rising push by hyper MAGA authorities across the country to turn back the freedoms we should not take for granted," White House press secretary Karine Jean-Pierre said in a statement, alluding to Trump supporters' "Make America Great Again" slogan.

The Oklahoma abortion providers' ability to execute procedures had already been severely limited by the six-week abortion restriction. The governor's signing on the law enacted Thursday, according to Andrea Gallegos, executive administrator at the Tulsa Women's Clinic, would make performing any abortions in the state impossible.

Ms. Gallegos stated, "These restrictions do not prevent abortion." "Women will continue to seek and receive abortions." We're simply forcing citizens of this country to flee their states to get health care. It's a disaster."

Abortion rights supporters warned that the consequences might be felt across the country.

"Overturning Roe vs. Wade would not only be the outcome of decades of a hateful campaign against women's rights; it would also be deeply racist and classist," Amnesty International Secretary General Agnes Callamard said in response to reports that the Supreme Court is preparing to overturn abortion rights in the United States.

Any decision to ban safe and legal abortion would disproportionately harm women of color and the poor. If the Supreme Court overturns Roe vs. Wade, it will be demonstrating a complete disregard for extensive evidence of the life-threatening consequences of criminalizing abortion and the resulting number of deaths from unsafe abortion. As a result, such a decision would be a violation of both the right to life and the prohibition against torture.

While recent moves to decriminalize and legalize abortion in Argentina, Ireland, Mexico, and Colombia have been huge victories for the international community, there are troubling signs that the United States is falling behind the rest of the world in terms of protecting sexual and reproductive rights. US government should safeguard the right to legal and safe abortion as anything less would be a blatant violation of human rights, which include the rights to life, health, physical autonomy, privacy, and dignity.

Any reversal in the protection of the right to abortion would not only harm the United States' international reputation; it would also set a terrible precedent that other governments and anti-rights groups could use to deny the rights of women, girls, and other people who can become pregnant around the world. Overturning Roe v. Wade would be the signal of a global backlash, jeopardizing recent gains and putting the health and lives of millions in jeopardy."

"This sends a message to other states that they, too, can prohibit abortion," said Elizabeth Nash, a Guttmacher Institute state policy specialist. "And it interrupts access across the country for our clinic network."

The Oklahoma bill would allow civilian lawsuits against anyone who assists in the payment of an abortion, potentially implicating people across the country who donate to charitable groups that help women in restrictive states obtain abortions abroad. Those who win their lawsuit will receive at least $10,000 in damages, as well as compensatory damages, such as for "emotional distress."

The bill exempts women who undergo abortions from lawsuits, which has been a sticking point in legislatures. It does not apply to abortions performed "in a medical emergency" to preserve the mother's life.

Bills prohibiting abortion beginning at fertilization have been argued by proponents of abortion rights to effectively ban contraceptive methods that prevent implantation, such as an intrauterine device, but the Oklahoma bill specifically states that it does not apply to contraception, such as Plan B or morning-after pills.

3

IMPACT OF ABORTION RESTRICTION ON WOMEN'S HEALTH AND RIGHT

Limiting women's access to safe and legal abortion services has serious health consequences. We've observed that these laws have little effect on the number of abortions performed. Rather, they force women to put their lives and health at risk by seeking hazardous abortion treatment.

According to the World Health Organization, 23,000 women die each year as a result of improper abortions, with tens of thousands more suffering serious health consequences. According to a recent study, outlawing abortion in the United States would result in a 21% rise in overall pregnancy-related mortality and a 33% increase among Black women, simply because staying pregnant is riskier than getting an abortion. Additional deaths from unsafe abortions or attempted abortions would be included in these figures.

If the current trend in the United States continues, "back alley" abortions will become the only option for women who lack access to safe and legal abortions, and the horrific consequences of such abortions will become a major cause of death and serious health complications for some of the country's most vulnerable women.

Abortion's legal status also determines whether girls will be able to finish their educations and whether women will be able to work and participate in public and political life.

Improving women's social safety net programs closes gender inequalities, improves girls' and women's health and increases their chances of reaching their full potential, all while potentially lowering the number of abortions. Women who are better educated, have better access to comprehensive reproductive health care, and are working and decently compensated will be better positioned to avoid unintended pregnancy, reducing the need for abortion.

Should Abortion Be Regarded As A Fundamental Human Right?

The right to safe and legal abortion is protected as a fundamental human right in numerous international and regional human rights treaties and national constitutions around the world. Safe abortion is part of a package of rights that includes the rights to life, liberty, privacy, equality and non-discrimination, and freedom from harsh, inhuman and degrading treatment. Restrictive abortion regulations have been regularly denounced by human rights organizations as being incompatible with human rights norms.

While a supporting legislative framework for abortion care is essential, it is insufficient to ensure that everyone who needs abortion care has access. Policies that pay the expense of abortion care and integrate it into the healthcare system, as well as societal efforts that de-stigmatize the operation, are required for universal access to become a reality.

A medical operation that terminates a pregnancy is known as an abortion. For millions of women, girls, and those who may become pregnant, it is a basic healthcare requirement. Every year, about one in every four pregnancies in the world ends in an abortion. While the necessity for abortion is prevalent, persons who require abortion services may not always have access to safe and legal abortion services. In truth, abortion access is one of the most contentious issues in the world, with disinformation about the true consequences of restricting access to this vital healthcare service clouding the debate.

Reproductive Rights And Maternal Health

Amnesty International affirms that any woman, girl, or person who has the potential to become pregnant has the right to an abortion, given that their rights, autonomy, dignity, and needs are respected in the context of their lived experiences, circumstances, aspirations, and opinions. Amnesty International's abortion policy calls for the complete decriminalization of abortion, as well as universal access to abortion, post-abortion care, and evidence-based, non-biased abortion-related information that is free of coercion, violence, and discrimination. The organization's abortion policy is founded on international human rights law and norms, as well as long-standing human rights ideals.

The following are the most important aspects of Amnesty International's abortion policy:

1. Every pregnant woman, girl, or person has the right to an abortion, given that their dignity, autonomy, and needs are respected in the context of their living circumstances, experiences, aspirations, and perspectives.

Every pregnant person should be able to make pregnancy decisions based on their own life experiences, circumstances, aspirations, and perspectives. They need non-biased and non-directive counseling, as well as any required support to enable autonomous decision-making.

Abortions must be carried out freely and without compulsion, violence, or prejudice, as well as without the necessity for third-party permission or the threat of legal action.

No one should be forced to seek or have an unsafe abortion, or to die or suffer needlessly as a result of unsafe abortion.

No one should be treated unfairly, humiliated, degraded, or face violence or social exclusion as a result of seeking or having an abortion. Because of pregnancy or, more broadly, because of their sex, sexual orientation, gender, gender identity or expression, age, race, geographic location, nationality, ethnicity, caste, class, disability, migrant or refugee status, and minority or Indigenous identity, among other factors, no one's full status as a rights holder and equal subject before the law can be suspended, diminished, or mandatorily set aside.

2. Abortion and post-abortion care should be readily available, inexpensive, acceptable, and of high quality.

They should be delivered with informed consent and with respect for pregnant women's rights, autonomy, dignity, privacy, and secrecy. States must ensure that abortions are available as early as possible and as late as necessary to meet the individual needs of pregnant women.

So that pregnant women may not feel driven to take undue risks to end their pregnancies, abortion care should be readily available, accepted, affordable, and of high quality.

Provision of abortion services with informed consent that respects the rights, autonomy, dignity, privacy, and secrecy of pregnant women.

Medical (abortion pill) and surgical abortion techniques that are easily accessible and meet the particular needs of pregnant women are based on evidence-based guidelines.

To assure access to abortion treatment, particularly in remote and rural areas, a variety of settings (for example, official healthcare settings; primary, secondary, and tertiary healthcare centers; mobile clinics; and telemedicine) and educated physicians are needed.

Regardless of the legality of abortion, people who are dealing with complications from a miscarriage or abortion should have access to post-abortion care; regulate refusals of care for lawful services (including based on conscience); and prohibit the denial of such care on any grounds, including conscience or beliefs.

Access to comprehensive sexual and reproductive health services, goods, and information, while respecting the autonomy, dignity, privacy, and confidentiality of pregnant women, as well as their human rights.

Pregnant women should have equitable access to sexual and reproductive health care, including abortion and post-abortion care, contemporary contraceptives, and evidence-based, non-biased information, including information about their pregnancy. That healthcare providers receive training on how to provide compassionate and ethical abortion, post-abortion care, and miscarriage therapy. This should include education on the social determinants of abortion, as well as ethical and acceptable care. Health-care personnel should be trained on pertinent abortion laws and policies, as well as the rights of all people who may become pregnant.

3. States have a positive responsibility to provide an environment that allows people to make informed decisions about their pregnancies.

States must ensure that everyone who is pregnant or may become pregnant has the freedom to make their own pregnancy-related decisions. This should include the right to have access to evidence-based, non-biased, accessible, and rights-based information and support regarding their pregnancy, without the need for a third-party approval.

States must remove obstacles to access to safe abortion care. Financial, social, geographic, detention-related, and disability-related barriers (for example, physical barriers, lack of access to evidence-based, non-biased information and discriminatory attitudes, and substituted decision-making by a guardian) are among the laws, policies, and practices that prevent pregnant people from accessing safe abortion services.

States may regulate abortion access, including by imposing gestational limits, according to Amnesty International, but gestational limits, like all other restrictions, should not be considered acceptable by default. Instead, a human rights study of the legal, legislative, and other regulatory measures on abortion in a specific country and setting, based on human rights principles, should be conducted to determine the impact of the restrictions on the human rights of pregnant people.

This involves providing free or low-cost services to ensure that individuals and families are not disproportionately burdened by healthcare costs, and low-income persons should be given the assistance they need to afford the costs. States must recognize, regardless of mental capacity, the legal capacity of women, girls, and pregnant people with disabilities to make autonomous decisions regarding sexuality, reproduction, and pregnancy, and must provide any required support to enable such informed and autonomous decision-making.

States should take steps to guarantee that no one is forced to maintain a pregnancy or have an abortion, whether as a result of human rights abuses such as gender or intersectional discrimination, or limits on abortion access.

States shall guarantee that all persons have access to evidence-based, age-appropriate, gender-sensitive, and human rights-based comprehensive sexuality education (CSE), both in and out of school settings. CSE programs should promote gender equality and prevent reinforcing stereotypes based on gender, sexual orientation, or other factors. CSE programs must also take into consideration children's and teenagers' changing capacities and provide them with the knowledge and skills they need to make informed and independent decisions.

States must identify and address the underlying factors that foster and promote gender, racial, ethnic, class, disability, and other intersecting forms of discrimination that contribute to reproductive oppression, promote and perpetuate restrictive and punitive abortion regulations, and fuel stigma and discrimination against people who have sought or obtained abortions, or are presumed to have done so.

States must address the stigma surrounding sexuality, sex, disability, unwanted pregnancies, and abortion, which obstruct sexual and reproductive autonomy, limits access to safe abortion, creates and perpetuates gender inequality, and facilitates ableism.

States must ensure that pregnant women have accurate, non-biased information about and access to services and support, such as health care, social security, and the means to achieve an adequate standard of living so that they are empowered to make free decisions about whether to carry their pregnancy to term, in line with their life aspirations and views and that they are not compelled to seek abortion due to denial of their economic and social rights.

4. Abortion must be made completely legal.

States must make abortion completely legal (that is, remove abortion from criminal law). They must also repeal any laws or policies, as well as any practices, that directly or indirectly penalize anyone who seeks, acquire, provide, or help in getting an abortion.

Anyone who seeks or obtains, or is suspected of seeking or obtaining, an abortion; health-care providers who facilitate or provide abortion medication or services; and others who assist or in any way help people obtain abortion medication or services must not be punished through the enforcement of any law or policy. All individuals who have been imprisoned for having an abortion, miscarriage, or another pregnancy-related problem, or for having purchased abortion drugs, must be released immediately. Health-care providers must be treated similarly.

Sexuality, sexual and reproductive health, human rights and empowerment, non-discrimination, gender equality and gender roles, sexual behavior, sexual abuse, gender-based violence, and harmful behaviors should all be covered in such education.

"Ableism" is described as discrimination or prejudice against people with disabilities or discrimination in favor of people who are able-bodied (Merriam-Webster Dictionary) (Oxford English Dictionary).

Abortion should be decriminalized completely to respect, defend, and fulfill the human rights of all people who can become pregnant. It is not, however, sufficient in and of itself; it must be complemented by governments' other positive commitments linked to abortion, which are highlighted throughout this policy.

5. The human rights compliance of all legal, policy and regulatory systems around abortion should be examined.

In developing laws and policies to regulate abortion and remove abortion-related stigma and discrimination, states must emphasize the concerns, lived experiences, and human rights of women, girls, and all persons who can become pregnant. By their right to full, effective, and meaningful participation in law and policymaking on issues that affect their lives, states must ensure that women, girls, and people who may become pregnant are adequately consulted and can meaningfully participate in the formulation, monitoring, and evaluation of abortion-related laws and policies.

Abortion-related legal, policy and regulatory frameworks should be evaluated to ensure that they respect and defend the human rights of women, girls, and all persons who may become pregnant. The impact on the rights to life, health, privacy, education, access to evidence-based, accurate information and the advantages of scientific advancement, freedom of conscience, freedom from torture and other ill-treatment, and equality and non-discrimination should all be included in the assessment.

States must reform all legal, policy, and regulatory frameworks that deal with abortion or have an impact on pregnancy-related decision-making to ensure that: the sexual and reproductive autonomy of women, girls, and all people who can become pregnant is at the center; pregnant people's human rights are respected, protected, and fulfilled; and gender equality and economic and social rights are realized.

Human rights protection, including the right to life, begins at birth. While states may have a genuine interest in preserving maternal and fetal health, abortion should not be subject to criminal or punitive legislation, and abortion-related legislation should not grant legal rights to gametes, zygotes, embryos, or fetuses.

According to research and data, the greatest way to safeguard fetal health is to promote the health and well-being of pregnant women and to have non-criminalized legal and regulatory contexts.

States must guarantee that women, girls, and individuals who may become pregnant have timely access to justice and meaningful and effective remedies when their sexual and reproductive rights are violated, including legal assistance and information about such remedies. When third parties infringe on people's sexual and reproductive rights, authorities must ensure that such violations are investigated, perpetrators are held accountable, and those who were harmed are compensated.

As part of states' overarching obligations to respect, protect, and fulfill the human rights of all people, Amnesty International's abortion policy reflects state obligations to realize sexual and reproductive rights and enable reproductive justice for women and girls, as well as all people who can become pregnant. This includes decriminalizing abortion completely and ensuring that no one, including pregnant women, health-care providers, or others, faces criminal or punitive consequences for seeking or having (or being presumed to have sought or had) an abortion, performing an abortion, or assisting others in obtaining or performing an abortion.

States must also ensure that all pregnant individuals have access to abortion, post-abortion care, and evidence-based, non-biased abortion-related information, as part of comprehensive sexual and reproductive health services, goods, and information.

Abortion should be made legal, policy, administrative, economic, social, cultural, and other barriers to be removed. States must also work to combat abortion-related stigma, harmful stereotyping, gender, and intersectional discrimination, which are at the root of abortion criminalization and other restrictive abortion laws and policies. They must also promote social, economic, and health policies that enable individuals to make autonomous and informed choices about their sexual and reproductive lives.

4

INTERNATIONAL HUMAN RIGHTS ORGANIZATIONS' ROLE IN ADVOCATING FOR LEGAL REFORM

In recent years, a new layer of involvement in abortion advocacy has evolved, based on an investigation of how existing laws affect women and girls and whether they follow international human rights norms. The Human Rights Committee, the Committee on the Elimination of Discrimination Against Women, the Committee on Economic, Social, and Political Rights, the Working Group on Discrimination Against Women in Law and Practice, and the Special Rapporteurs on the right to the highest attainable standard of health, women's rights in Africa, and torture have all become increasingly vocal in calling for progressive abortion laws.

The Inter-American Court of Human Rights, the European Court of Human Rights, and the African Commission on Human and Peoples' Rights (ACHPR) have all been active in this area. In January 2016, the African Commission on Human Rights (ACHPR) called for the decriminalization of abortion across Africa, in accordance with the Maputo Protocol, and renewed that call in January 2017, causing a stir across the continent.

Interestingly, no human rights organization has called for abortion to be legalized at the request of the woman, even though many have called for it to be decriminalized. This begs the question of what the phrase "decriminalization" means to different people.

The international abortion rights movement has always advocated for "safe, legal abortion." More recently, there have been efforts for the "decriminalization of abortion." Do these terms have the same meaning? In simple words, legalizing abortion implies retaining abortion in the law in some form by establishing the reasons for its legalization, but decriminalizing abortion involves abolishing all criminal sanctions against abortion.

In that sense, abortion is lawful in all but a few nations today on one or more grounds (usually as exceptions to the law), with Canada standing out as the only country to date to have effectively decriminalized abortion by a Supreme Court judgment in 1988. No other country, regardless of how liberal its legal reforms are, has been willing to remove abortion entirely from the law. This distinction, however, is not always made. Instead, the two phrases are used interchangeably, implying that abortion can be legalized or decriminalized for any or all reasons. No one is likely to be able to modify the terminology's lack of difference. However, it is critical to be explicit about what is and is not intended when suggesting abortion law reform.

Criminal prohibitions on abortion are found in statute law, which refers to legislation enacted by legislatures, frequently as part of criminal or penal codes that combine several criminal statutes. Abortion was made illegal in the United Kingdom (but not Northern Ireland) in sections 58 and 59 of the Offences against the Person Act of 1861, with one aspect further defined in the Infant Life Preservation Act of 1929, and then legalized on certain grounds and conditions in the 1967 Abortion Act, which was then amended further in the Human Fertilization and Embryology Act of 1990. Legal justifications for abortion are listed as exceptions to the criminal law in the 1967 Abortion Act, but the 1861 act is still in effect and is used to punish unlawful abortions today.

Ireland, which was once part of the United Kingdom, was similarly subject to the 1861 Offences against the Person Act, which was finally repealed in 2013 with the Protection of Life during Pregnancy Act, which enforced its own nearly comprehensive criminalization of abortion. Sierra Leone, a former British colony, repealed the 1861 Offences against Person Act in the Safe Abortion Act, which was passed overwhelmingly in December 2015 and again in February 2016. That act, which enables abortion on demand throughout the first 12 weeks of pregnancy and until week 24 in circumstances of rape, incest, or danger to the fetus' or woman's or girl's health, was never signed into law.

Abortion was lawful in 98 percent of the world's countries at the turn of the twentieth century to save a woman's life. Other reasons for abortion were: to protect a woman's physical health (63 percent); protect a woman's mental health (62 percent); in cases of rape, sexual abuse, or incest (43 percent); fetal abnormality or disability (39 percent); economic or social reasons (33 percent); and on request (27 percent).

In 2002, the number of countries that allowed each of these reasons varied dramatically by region. Thus, abortion was legal on-demand in 65% of affluent nations but only 14% of developing countries, and for economic and social reasons in 75% of developed countries but only 19% of developing countries. Additional grounds for abortion are allowed in some countries, such as if the woman has HIV, is under the age of 16 or over the age of 40, is not married, or has a large family. A few authorize it to protect existing children or because contraception has failed.

Uganda is a good example. Uganda's Constitution and Penal Code are incompatible, resulting in confusing interpretations and a lack of awareness that abortion is lawful to protect women's health and lives. Furthermore, while Uganda has a national reproductive health policy, it is neither legally backed nor executed. The minister of health and other stakeholders developed Standards and Evidence-based Guidelines on the Prevention of Unsafe Abortion in 2015 to clarify the situation. Details on who can perform abortions, where and how, and allocated health-care responsibilities, such as degree of care and post-abortion care, were among them. However, due to religious and political opposition, the rules were rescinded in January 2016.

Since it was approved in the International Conference on Population and Development's Programme of Action in 1994 as a stopgap measure to save lives, post-abortion care to treat the consequences of unsafe abortions has been implemented in countries where there was little or no prospect of law reform. However, in African nations such as Tanzania, where the 1981 Revised Penal Code leaves it unclear if abortion is lawful to preserve a woman's physical or mental health or life, and where unsafe abortions still account for 16 percent of maternal fatalities, this has not been a success.

Despite the government's efforts to increase post-abortion care access, a 2015 research revealed that "substantial gaps still existed, and most women were not receiving the care they needed." Following recent reports of doctors in both public and private hospitals accepting payments for performing abortions and a reported increase in cases of complications, the newly appointed prime minister, in tandem with the president, threatened to dismiss and possibly imprison doctors performing illegal abortions, according to a CCTV-Africa report.

Other restrictions that are unrelated to abortion might sometimes act as roadblocks. Morocco's abortion law was enacted in 1920, while the country was still French territory. A reform process to expand legal protections was launched in May 2015, following a public debate sparked by accounts of women dying as a result of unsafe abortion. Unmarried women would be excluded because it is illegal to have sex outside of marriage, according to the Moroccan Family Planning Association, despite a consensus that abortion should be permitted within the first three months if the woman's physical and mental health is in danger and cases of rape, incest, or congenital malformation.

In 1971, India passed a highly permissive abortion law for the time, but it was poorly and unevenly executed, resulting in high rates of morbidity and mortality that persist to this day. Even 15 years ago, registering a clinic as a licensed abortion provider was a time-consuming process that limited the number of facilities. Furthermore, two other laws have hampered abortion access: the Pre-Conception and Pre-Natal Diagnostic Techniques (Prohibition of Sex Selection) Act, which prohibits the use of ultrasound for sex determination and has resulted in restrictions on all second-trimester abortions, and the Protection of Children from Sexual Offenses Act, which requires reporting of underage sex and makes minors who become pregnant feel unsafe if they seek an abortion.

Without altering the legislation itself, decent laws and policies can be sabotaged, and access to abortion can be curtailed through policies urging women to have more children, public condemnation of abortion by political and religious leaders, or limiting access to services. Unnecessary medical tests, counseling even if women do not feel they need it, having to get one or more doctors' signatures, having to wait between making an appointment and having an abortion, or having to obtain consent from a partner, parent(s), guardian, or even a judge may be placed in women's paths.

In Turkey, for example, the government passed a law in 1983 to regulate fertility, allow for abortion up to 10 weeks after conception, and sterilize in response to population growth. Before the procedure, a married woman seeking an abortion only needed to obtain her husband's permission or submit a formal statement of assumption of all responsibility. President Erdogan, on the other hand, has taken a pronatalist position in recent years, urging Turkish couples to have at least three children. He has been calling abortion murder since 2012, expressing opposition to abortion services, and threatening to change the law. Women protested in such great numbers in 2012 in response to these threats that the statute has remained unchanged to this day. However, administrative modifications were made to make scheduling an abortion appointment—which is still predominantly performed by gynecologists in hospitals—more difficult.

These regulations have made getting an abortion in a public hospital nearly hard; in fact, several state hospitals have stopped performing abortions entirely. As a result, the availability of safe abortion is contingent not only on liberal legislation, but also on a permissive atmosphere, political support, and the ability and willingness of health services and health professionals to provide abortion. Ethiopia, in contrast to Turkey, is an example of that support's success.

Ethiopia liberalized its abortion laws in 2005. Abortion was formerly only permitted to save a woman's life or to protect her physical condition. Abortion is legal in cases of rape, incest, or fetal impairment, as well as if the woman's life or physical health is in danger, if she has a physical or mental disability, or if she is a minor who is physically or mentally unprepared for childbirth. This is a liberal law for Sub-Saharan Africa, but little was known about its execution for a long time.

According to a 2011 study by Jemila Abdi and Mulugeta Gebremariam, Ethiopian health care providers' reasons for not performing abortions were primarily personal or owing to a lack of consent from an employer, or the lack of resources at their facility. Only 27% of respondents said they felt safe working in an abortion clinic. Religious reasons were the most common, but personal values and a lack of training also played a role.

While a significant number of abortions are still performed outside of health institutions, the proportion is decreasing, indicating that change is feasible but requires time. A mix of legal reforms, court judgments, and public health standards have improved women's access to safe abortion in Latin America in recent decades. Allowing abortion on demand in the first trimester of pregnancy, like in Mexico City (since 2007) and Uruguay, is one of them (since 2012). Higher courts in Argentina, Bolivia, Brazil, Colombia, and Costa Rica have played a key role in assessing the validity and breadth of certain abortion grounds, however, their decisions are not always followed. Guidelines published by hospitals or federal or state governments govern the enforcement of approved grounds in nations like Peru. Additional steps are required, as Ethiopia has demonstrated, which include training clinicians and ensuring that services deliver legal abortions, as well as notifying women about the changes and options available.

Despite more than 30 years of battles for women's sexual and reproductive rights and human rights in other Latin American countries, abortion laws have remained extremely restricted. As a result, and thanks to advancements in technology, women have begun to take control of their lives. Since its abortifacient effectiveness was first discovered in the late 1980s, an untold number of women, likely in the millions, have been obtaining and using misoprostol to self-induce abortion (widely available for gastric ulcers) from a variety of sources—pharmacies, websites, and the black market

This tradition, which originated in Brazil, has since spread to a number of other countries and areas. In an attempt to halt the inevitable, countries including Brazil and Egypt have implemented legal restrictions and regulations on access to medical abortion pills.

Furthermore, feminist organizations such as Women Help Women, Women on Web, safe2choose, the Tabbot Foundation in Australia, and TelAbortion in the United States have established safe abortion information hotlines in at least 20 countries in the last decade, and health professionals are providing information and access to abortion pills via telemedicine.

While the global trend is toward more progressive policies, several countries where the right has gained power have regressed. From 1931 through 1989, Chilean law permitted abortion on therapeutic grounds, which was defined as "termination of a pregnancy before the fetus becomes viable to preserve the mother's life or safeguard her health" in the Penal Code. As he departed office in 1989, Pinochet, the dictator who ousted the Allende administration, outlawed abortion, leaving no legal basis for it. n Michelle Bachelet's government did not introduce a bill allowing three grounds for legal abortion until 2016, during her second term in office—to save the woman's life, in cases of rape or sexual abuse, and in cases of a fatal fetal anomaly—which are narrower than what was in place between 1931 and 1989 but are the best that supporters believe they can get.

With each change of the head of state in Russia, the law has shifted from permissive to restrictive. When Stalin took over from Lenin, he made abortion illegal, but after 1945, abortion was once again legal on broad grounds throughout the Soviet Union and its satellite countries in Eastern Europe and West Asia, while Vladimir Putin has imposed a long list of restrictions, greatly reducing the number of grounds on which abortion is legal. In January 2016, a bill was introduced in parliament with the goal of "preventing the unrestricted use of pharmaceutical medications intended for pregnancy termination." It would have prohibited retail sales and restricted the kind of organizations that might purchase medical abortion pills in bulk.

Abortions in private clinics would be prohibited, and reimbursement for them would be eliminated from state insurance coverage. It also would not have permitted abortions to be funded by state health insurance unless the woman's life was in danger. The law was dropped following widespread public outcry, which was orchestrated by the Russian Association for Population and Development; however, further restrictions are likely to be implemented.

The backlash against the communist government in several Central and Eastern European countries, along with the growing influence of conservative religious figures, has resulted in repeated attempts to weaken abortion regulations. Poland has been hit the hardest. In 1993, a liberal law was repealed, leaving only three legal grounds for abortion: a serious threat to the pregnant woman's life or health, as attested by two physicians; cases of rape or incest if confirmed by a prosecutor; and cases in which antenatal tests, as attested by two physicians, demonstrated that the fetus was seriously and irreversibly damaged. Despite an attempt to outlaw all abortions in 2016, thanks to months of nationwide activity by women's groups, including a national women's strike on October 3, 2016, this law remains in place.

In November 2016, the government enacted a rule that allows pregnant women carrying a severely handicapped or unviable fetus to receive a one-time payment of €1,000 to continue the pregnancy to term, even if the baby would be delivered dead or die soon after delivery. Access to hospice and medical treatment, psychological counseling, baptism or blessing, burial, and a person who will function as an "assistant to the family" and coordinate the support are all included in the package. The stated goal was to limit the number of legal abortions due to fetal abnormalities.

This heinous proposal, vile anti-abortion propaganda, and systematic pressure on hospitals in Poland to stop performing abortions on medical grounds exemplify the anti-abortion movement's right-wing extremism today, whose epicenter is in the United States and whose war on women can feel unending at times.

However, this does not prevent women from having abortions.

With a law that remains unique in Latin America and the Caribbean, Cuba was the first country to alter its abortion law in favor of women. Abortion has been provided through the national health system on demand up to the tenth week of pregnancy since 1965. According to the Penal Code, abortion is only prohibited if it is performed without the pregnant woman's consent, is dangerous, or is performed for profit.

The law enabling abortion in Japan, adopted in 1948, was initially based on eugenics, but in practice was a liberal law. Abortion became the country's major method of birth control as a result of this regulation. In 1996, the statute was changed to remove all references to eugenics. Abortion is currently legal for health grounds, including socioeconomic reasons, and sexual offenses. Abortion was and still is the most common method of controlling fertility. The vast majority of abortions are classified as medically necessary. Abortions are almost always performed during the first trimester.

In recent years, public health statutes, judicial rulings, and policies and regulations on sexual and reproductive health care, rather than criminal law, have been used to legalize abortion in several countries. Uruguay's 2012 law is an example of public health legislation that establishes processes and health-care standards for abortion services.

The Luxembourg parliament decided in December 2014 to remove abortion from the Penal Code up to 12 weeks of pregnancy, and to remove the need that the woman is "in distress" owing to her pregnancy. Regulations governing who can perform abortions have also been updated. In France, the 1975 Veil Law was modified in 2014, 2015, and 2016 to expand abortion access and remove impediments. In France, women no longer need to be in a "state of anguish," but just need to request an abortion. The obligatory seven-day "reflection period" between the abortion request and the actual abortion was also eliminated. Most recently, midwives have been permitted to perform medical abortions, and all abortion costs have been paid.

Sweden's law is one of the most liberal in the world, however, abortion is not completely legal. In 1938, 1946, 1963, 1975, 1995, 2007, and 2008, the Swedish law was changed. Abortion is available up to 18 weeks on request. The National Board of Health and Welfare must then approve approval, which may or may not be granted if the fetus is viable. It is not possible to appeal. Abortion providers and locations are regulated. Anyone who conducts an abortion on another person who is not licensed to practice medicine faces a fine or a year in prison. The government subsidizes abortion; 95% of abortions happen before 12 weeks, and nearly none after 18 weeks. The majority of abortions are medical.

Each state and the Australian Capital Territory has its own set of laws, ranging from quite liberal to extremely stringent; several are now being revised. The Supreme Court of the United States ruled in 1973 that criminalizing abortion violated a woman's right to privacy and that abortion should be a joint decision between her and her doctor. The court did, however, rule that the US governments have an interest in protecting pregnant women's safety and well-being, as well as the possibility of human life. This opened the door to further restrictions as the pregnancy progressed, allowing states to implement limits that are still tying up state and federal courts to this day. It's impossible not to believe that no law is the best law when it comes to abortion, which brings us back to Canada, where abortion has been legal since 1988 and is available on-demand with no restrictions on who must do it or where it must be performed. Despite the fact that abortion is difficult to obtain in rural regions and Canada took an unusually long time to approve mifepristone, anti-abortion sentiment has never gained traction. The advantages of having no law for women are obvious.

Although recent efforts for abortion legalization by human rights organizations, lawmakers, and feminist groups aim to decriminalize only particular grounds and conditions related to abortion, this is still better than nothing. Thus, in Chile, El Salvador, Honduras, and Peru, where abortion is illegal, requests to "decriminalize abortion" are limited to three to four reasons: to safeguard the woman's life and health, to treat serious or fatal fetal defects, and to prevent rape or sexual abuse. While these are not the most common reasons for abortion, they are the only ones that have a possibility of gaining majority support through legislative reform in situations where "everything" is just not possible.

At its core, the degree of decriminalization desired reflects the amount to which abortion is regarded as a legitimate form of health care—not just by proponents of the right to safe abortion, but also by politicians, health professionals, the media, and the general public. The fact that abortion is illegal in practically all countries is not only a historical relic, but also a reflection of widespread ambivalence and negativity toward abortion in most societies, regardless of how old or where the law originated.

Some abortion-rights proponents appear to be concerned that if anything is not left in the criminal law, "terrible things" may begin to happen. Canada demonstrates that this is not the case. Granted, Canada isn't everywhere. However, there are basic criminal rules that allow misbehavior to be punished, such as forcing a woman to have an abortion against her will, providing her medical abortion drugs without her knowledge, or injuring or killing her through a dangerous operation. These are statutes against causing serious physical damage, assault, or manslaughter that can be used without the necessity for abortion-related criminal legislation.

It takes years to successfully change the law on abortion. Advocates do not have many opportunities to modify the legislation, so they must decide what they want to achieve before lobbying for it, confident that whatever they suggest will be adopted. Another chance may not be available anytime soon.

Allies are really important. Parliamentarians, health professionals, legal experts, women's organizations and organizations, human rights organizations, proponents of family planning, and, most all, women themselves are crucial. Obtaining a critical mass of support from all of these groups, as well as defeating the opposition, which can exert influence beyond its numbers, is important to successful legislative reform.

Those who are unable to consider no law at all must address the fact that each legal ground for abortion can be read liberally or narrowly, resulting in different implementations in different situations, or no implementation at all. The difficulty is determining which abortions should remain illegal and how they should be punished. Even if only some justifications are admissible, while amending existing law, the question of who decides and on what basis remains.

Millions of women and several abortion providers violate restrictive abortion regulations regularly. Even in countries with more liberal laws, research reveals that the letter of the law is being bent in a variety of ways to meet women's needs. Despite this, opposition and a dogged refusal to act continue to stymie efforts to meet women's unrestricted abortion needs.

It should be obvious that the multitude of complicated abortion rules and limitations make no legal or public health sense. What makes abortion safe is that it is provided at the desire of the mother and is universally affordable and accessible. Few existing laws are fit for purpose from this perspective, as they simply repeat every possible permutation of the same restrictions.

Here's What's Going On In Certain US States:

MISSISSIPPI ISLAND – The alleged leak is a draft judgment in a case brought by Mississippi, which wants to reinstate a rule that prohibits abortions after 15 weeks of pregnancy. A lower court has struck down the law. By the end of June, the Supreme Court is anticipated to make a verdict. Mississippi officials had urged the Supreme Court to reverse the Roe v. Wade decision, as well as a 1992 decision prohibiting regulations that imposed an "undue hardship" on abortion access.

OKLAHOMA CITY — On May 3 2022, Oklahoma Governor Kevin Stitt signed a bill prohibiting abortion after six weeks of pregnancy, effectively making abortion illegal in the state. It is based on a restriction enacted in neighboring Texas last year that is enforced through civil litigation. Oklahoma has already become a popular abortion destination for women from Texas.

Several anti-abortion laws have been approved by Oklahoma lawmakers, with the hope that at least one may survive court challenges. Stitt enacted another ban in April, which will take effect in August and could result in fines of up to $100,000 and ten years in prison for abortion providers.

TEXAS – In September, Texas made news when it passed a near-total abortion ban. It is one of several Republican states that have passed "heartbeat" abortion bans, which prohibit abortions after a fetal heartbeat is found, usually at six weeks, which is before most women realize they are pregnant.

Rape and incest are not immune from the law. Citizens in Texas have the uncommon authority to sue doctors who perform abortions after the cut-off date. Citizens can receive $10,000 if their lawsuits are successful. This has been dubbed a "bounty" by President Joe Biden's administration. According to abortion rights organizations, 85 percent to 90 percent of abortions in Texas are obtained after six weeks, implying that many facilities will have to close.

FLORIDA Governor Ron DeSantis signed a measure prohibiting abortions beyond 15 weeks in April. They are presently permitted till the age of 24 weeks. Women in the southeast would have less access to late-term abortions under the new law, which takes effect on July 1. Because of tighter abortion restrictions in other states, many women travel hundreds of miles to end their pregnancies in Florida.

ARIZONA – In March, Republican Governor Doug Ducey signed a bill prohibiting abortion after 15 weeks unless it is medically necessary. For rape or incest, there are no exceptions. If the new law is not challenged in court, it will likely take effect by late summer.

KENTUCKY passed a broad anti-abortion bill in April that went into effect immediately, requiring abortion doctors to stop performing procedures unless they can meet certain conditions. Among them is a requirement that fetal remains be buried or interred. Clinics throughout the state say the regulations make it too difficult and expensive to operate. Kentucky officials have been temporarily prevented from enforcing the law by a federal judge.

IDAHO - In March, Republican Governor Brad Little enacted a six-week abortion ban, similar to that of Texas. It allows the family of the fetus to sue abortion doctors if a heartbeat is discovered during the procedure. The bill was set to take effect in April, but the state Supreme Court delayed it pending legal review.

SOUTH DAKOTA – In March, Republican Governor Kristi Noem signed a bill requiring women seeking medications for a medical abortion to attend a clinic three times to be evaluated and get medication. The execution of the legislation is contingent on the outcome of a federal court case.

WYOMING – Earlier this year, the state passed a "trigger ban," which would prohibit most abortions if the Supreme Court overturns Roe v. Wade. The bill would make exceptions in circumstances of life-threatening situations for women, as well as sexual assault and incest.

LOUISIANA – State legislators have adopted a prohibition similar to Mississippi's, but it will not go into effect until Mississippi's law is finalized.

ARKANSAS outlawed all abortions except in medical emergencies in March 2021, with no exceptions for cases of rape or incest. The prohibition has been put on hold while Planned Parenthood, the nation's largest abortion provider, and the American Civil Liberties Union filed a court challenge. The case is still pending in the courts.

MONTANA – The Republican-controlled legislature has enacted numerous legislation restricting abortion access, including one that prohibits terminations after 20 weeks of pregnancy. The laws have been put on hold while Planned Parenthood files a legal challenge.

In 2021, Republican Governor Henry McMaster enacted a law prohibiting abortion once a baby's heartbeat is found in South Carolina. A legal challenge by Planned Parenthood has put the bill on hold.

TENNESSEE – In 2020, the state passed sweeping legislation that included banning abortion as early as six weeks and requiring patients to be informed about the possibility of reversing medication abortions, despite the fact that many medical experts disagree. Due to a judicial challenge, the majority of the statute has been halted. However, there is a provision that prohibits abortions based on a Down's syndrome diagnosis.

OHIO - In 2021, a federal appeals court declared that Ohio can carry out a 2017 legislation prohibiting abortions when medical testing reveals a fetus has Down's syndrome. A bill requiring the cremation or burial of fetal tissue has also been approved in Ohio.

PENNSYLVANIA – Abortion providers lost a court battle in 2021 to overturn a limit on using state Medicaid payments for abortions. They've taken their case to the Pennsylvania Supreme Court.

CONCLUSION

How to Reduce Abortion the Right Way

Many centrist and progressive politicians have come to speak a reasonably consistent message regarding abortion during the last year. To disassociate themselves from the misconception that "Pro-Choice" = "abortion on demand," they have proposed a "moderate," "compromise" position: uphold Roe v. Wade while working to limit the number of abortions in the United States. Reducing the annual number of abortions, which currently stands at over 1 million, is a commendable aim. There are, however, other paths to that aim, some of which will benefit women and others which will not.

Simply said, there are two methods to limit abortion: make it less necessary or make it less accessible. Only the former method, in our opinion, is humane, effective, and just.

Those who oppose abortion in all or most instances believe that making it illegal is the greatest method to minimize the number of abortions. They believe that by making abortion illegal, it will become obsolete. They hold this belief despite overwhelming evidence that women continue to undergo abortions in countries where they are illegal and hazardous, sometimes resulting in tragic outcomes. Every year, almost 70,000 women die as a result of improper abortions, and many more suffer serious ailments such as infection, bleeding, and infertility. This harms women, their families, and entire communities, but it does not affect abortion rates.

Anti-abortion activists have yet to succeed in enacting a complete ban on abortion in the United States. As a result, they have worked hard to make it as inaccessible as possible. Anti-abortion activists have put safe and legal abortion out of reach for a significant segment of our population, namely the young, the rural, and, most importantly, the poor, by prohibiting public funding, increasing the cost with unnecessary clinic regulations, reducing the number of available doctors and clinics, imposing waiting periods, and mandating rigid parental involvement laws.

As a result, many women who have been denied Roe's safeguards have either been forced to carry and bear children against their will or have encountered enormous delays in obtaining an abortion, making the process more expensive, hazardous, emotionally, and ethically hard. Although making abortion illegal may lower the number of abortions, it does it brutally and unpleasantly.

The best strategy is to make abortion less necessary. The first step is to decrease the number of unplanned pregnancies. In this country, half of all pregnancies are unplanned, and half of those result in abortion. Unintended pregnancy may be considerably decreased if we made a genuine effort to:

1) comprehensive sexuality education, including medically accurate information about abstinence and contraception; 2) insurance coverage and public funding for family planning services; 3) increased access to emergency contraception (which prevents pregnancy but does not cause abortion), and 4) domestic violence and sexual abuse prevention programs. Women who can avoid an unplanned pregnancy do not have to face the tough option of whether or not to undergo an abortion.

Even with the above-mentioned resources, there will always be some unwanted pregnancies; birth control devices, like humans, are flawed. As a result, if a woman becomes pregnant unexpectedly, a second positive strategy to reduce abortion is to guarantee that she has the resources to have and raise a child in a healthy and safe environment if she so desires. One of the two most prevalent reasons women choose abortion, according to the Alan Guttmacher Institute, is that they cannot afford another child. Many low-income and young women would have the resources they need to fulfill the severe commitments that motherhood involves if they were provided with meaningful education and employment possibilities, health care, child care, housing, assistance for impaired children, and other fundamental supports.

Unfortunately, few of these policy goals are highlighted in today's abortion-reduction rhetoric. Instead, many centrist politicians have embraced the strategy of "splitting the difference," supporting some but not all of the limitations advocated by anti-abortion campaigners, such as biased counseling, bans on public funding, and prohibitions on certain abortion procedures. Even Democrats for Life's 95-10 initiative, which claims to have a plan to reduce abortions by 95% in ten years, provides only rudimentary support for pregnant women (funding for domestic violence programs and university daycare), no provision for birth control, and only oblique references to pregnancy prevention education.

These half-hearted attempts to reduce abortion are patently insufficient and appear to represent a watered-down "Pro-Life" goal rather than a true moderate, let alone progressive, objective.

Moderation for the sake of moderation and political compromise at the expense of women's rights will not achieve the common objective of reducing abortion in this country. What is required is leadership and commitment to a vision of society in which all women have access to the information and resources they need to avoid unintended pregnancies, carry healthy pregnancies to term, raise their children in a safe, stable, and dignified manner, and, yes, have safe abortions when necessary to live healthy, productive, and fulfilling lives.

The goal of this book was not to present answers or roadmaps, but each country's circumstances must be considered. The goal was to inspire new ways of thinking about whether a criminal ban against abortion is essential. Treating abortion as a form of essential health care is a significant step forward, and advocates could draft the simplest, most supportive law possible, putting first-trimester abortion care in primary and community settings, ensuring second-trimester services, involving mid-level providers, raising women's awareness of services and the law, aiming for universal access, incorporating WHO-approved methods, and addressing social asymmetry.

All criminal prohibitions against abortion would be repealed if it were up to me, making abortion available at the request of the only person who matters—the pregnant woman. Abortion, like all pregnancy care, would be free at the point of service and universally available from the beginning of pregnancy.

No criminal law is feasible or acceptable, as Canada has demonstrated. Sweden has demonstrated that with good services, abortions after 18 weeks can be effectively eliminated, and WHO has demonstrated that first-trimester abortions can be safely and effectively provided at the primary and community level by trained mid-level providers, as well as the provision of medical abortion pills by trained pharmacy workers. Finally, web- and phone-based telemedicine services are demonstrating that clinic-based services are not required to safely and successfully administer medical abortion pills. However, to attain these aims, or something near to them, a strong and active national coalition, as well as a critical mass of support, is required.

BIBLIOGRAPHY

Amnesty International Policy on Abortion; September 28 2020 Index number POL 30/2848/2020

Reuters, Guttmacher Institute, Center for American Progress, NARAL Pro-choice America, ACLU Reproductive Freedom Project, Kaiser Family Foundation

Forsthe, C. D (2013) Abuse of discretion: the inside story of Roe v. Wade. New York City. Encounter Books.

(2017) Arguments about Abortin: Parenthood, Morality and Law Oxford: Oxford University Press.